Table of Contents

Introduction 5

Awakening of Quantum Physics 9

The Unified Quantum Field 13

Creator, Created, Interaction 19

Introduction to Quantum Buddhism 23

About the Amitabha Sutra 27

The Conditioned Mind 29

Releasing the Mind 41

From Mind to Reality 49

The Formula 53

Emotional Transmutation 57

Conclusion 65

Introduction

Not so long ago (and maybe still in some parts of the world) religious, political and scientific power was held by the same people. Their goal was simple: to hold the truth. The Spiritual leaders were the deciders regarding just about everything. It was a time when new ideas coming out of new genius minds were set aflame... literally... at the stake. Fear from losing control was present in the leader's minds, as they used every possible means to keep the population away from thinking on their own. Their goal was to propagate a set of beliefs that encouraged us to behave along with the group, using what I like to call "persuasive armed marketing". The fundamental goal seemed to be good at the time, since it is important to maintain a good social structure. The difficulty arose when the individual feeling of freedom was hindered for the greater good of a few leaders, instead of the greater good of the entire group.

Science and religion have been opposed regarding consciousness since Descartes separated matter and mind. This separated view was named Cartesian Dualism. Since then, two non-dualist approaches to the world were developed. The first non-dualist view includes scientific materialism in which matter produces mind, from a series of mechanical reactions in the hormonal and nervous system, such as the brain. The second non-dualist view includes idealism, in which mind produces matter.

Buddhism (and neutral monists in western philosophy) believes that mind and matter both derive from a deeper-lying common entity. In recent decades it has become evident that quantum physics and quantum gravity can provide a scientifically plausible accommodation of the Buddhist (and neutral monist) approach.

In Buddhism the deeper-lying monistic entity is the pure wisdom of the Supreme Unified Consciousness which can give rise to matter and/or mind. In scientific terms it is the quantum geometry at the tiniest level (Planck scale) of the universe, which is called the *unified quantum field*. Cosmic wisdom of the Supreme Unified Consciousness pervades the universe, involving, informing and interconnecting everything, including living and non-living beings. It is everything. It is everywhere. Yet, this is only the perception we have from our human point of view. From the point of view of Supreme Consciousness, everything is at the same place, at the same time.

Universal wisdom could be seen as very small quantum information pervading the universe in a non-local and holographic way, hence repeating everywhere, atemporally (everywhen) and at various scales. We will see how we can practice ourselves to detach from the limited human perception of time and space, and practice at perceiving the higher wisdom, which is more refined than standard intellectual information.

In Buddhism, conscious awareness in an individual – self consciousness - is a series of ripples on the universal pond of the Supreme Unified Consciousness, interacting with the biological body, the nervous system, and thus, the senses. In science, self-consciousness is a series of quantum wave function reductions, ripples in quantum geometry on the edge between the quantum world of multiple coexisting possibilities, and the classical world of definite states, all occurring in the brain. It is nonetheless possible to become aware of this interaction between the pool of possibilities, and the world we believe to be definite and fixed.

Samadhi is a Sanskrit word describing awareness in which sensory inputs, memory and self dissolve, a person's consciousness becoming totally one with Supreme Unified Consciousness. Samadhi occurs during deep meditation. Scientifically, in altered states of consciousness, quantum brain activities may become more directly connected with the universal quantum geometry and its collective information.

Quantum Buddhism aims at providing a set of tools to develop a scientific-spiritual approach to the world, unburdened by traditional cultural ritualistic and dogmatic weight, where development of the self prevails to become a conscious scientific instrument. Along reading this book, you will learn a good basis of theory and application of this technique on transcending the human senses to perceive the spiritual world.

These techniques are the first steps in understanding beyond the human intellectual interpretation of the world, and existing beyond the biological body.

Spirit, mind, matter, and time are all the same from the point of view of the Supreme Consciousness. Every possibility exists. Every option is available. Yet, from the human point of view, only the result of the equations is perceived. With practice, you can become the mathematician, instead of the result of a formula. In fact, you will remember that you were always the creator of your own experience of life, but only awakened at the level where you perceive the end result of the experience.

In this new era of scientific and spiritual freedom, we can now try to answer age-old questions such as: What is life? Why is life? Why do we exist? What exists, exactly? How do we exist? The answers to all these questions are available at a level of consciousness that surpasses the ability of the human brain to compute these answers by itself. Thus, words cannot suffice to explain it. To find out these answers, one must thrive at discovering the truth by experiencing Supreme Consciousness thru meditative practices and to elevate the awareness of consciousness up to a spiritual level. From this new point of view, everything becomes so clear.

Awakening of Quantum Physics

While it is not the goal of this book to introduce the reader to quantum physics, we give here an overview, pointing directly at a specific phenomenon that interests us. Quantum physics is a very large field of study and you should make a bit more research if you are interested to go beyond the scope of this book. Therefore, this introduction will seem extremely brief for the purist. Here we will address a specific event where science discovered that there might be such a things as consciousness.

Quantum physics is the science of studying particles. Quantum is the Latin word for "how much". In a quest to identify and understand the smallest particles, below the scale of atoms, scientific research found out about a few wonderful phenomena that seem to happen only at the quantum scale. Particles, such as electrons, protons, neutrons and many others, behave differently if we pay attention to them or not.

There was a time, in traditional mechanical physics, that the subjects involved in an experiment were : 1- The experiment, 2- The instrument of measurement. But in quantum research, they noticed that the result of an experiment changed according to the way that the scientific people operating the experiment were involved in the experiment, and interacted with it.

In a summed up fashion, we will explain an experiment that used a subatomic particle cannon and receptive screen. The goal here is to give you the basic idea, and not to turn newcomers into scientific overlords.

This experiment is called the "double-slit" experiment. In a laboratory was used a subatomic particle cannon to shoot electrons at a receptive screen, after passing thru a filter plate with two tiny slits. While we would expect the electrons to draw two lines on the receptive screen, we saw a pattern that can only be explained if subatomic particles behave like waves.

Expected result

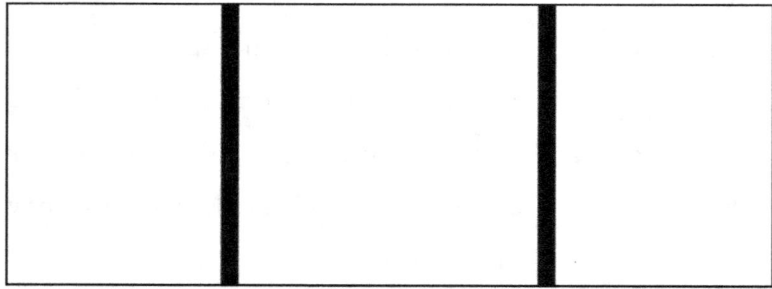

Actual wave-like result

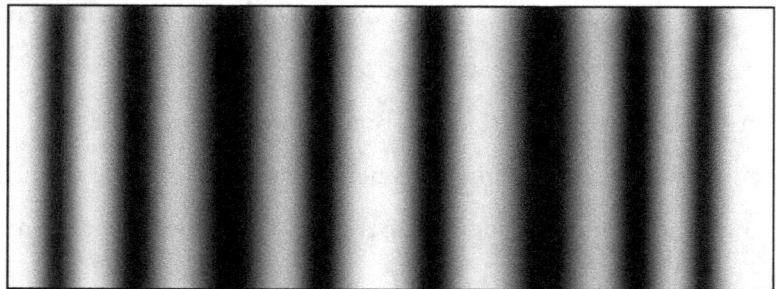

Thus, to understand the phenomenon, we must use measurement instrumentation to perceive what happens when the electrons pass thru the slits. At this point, when the operators of the scientific experiment used measuring devices to observe the electrons, these stopped behaving like waves and started to behave like particles.

Result while observing

Thus, it was deducted after many attempts to rule out any other possibility, that the observer had an influence on the experiment, and that he was actually part of it. When we observe a particle, where we put our attention on it, it becomes one of its possibilities, taking a definite position and form, but when we are not interacting with it, the particle holds all of its possibilities at once, in every position and form. Where once we considered two subjects involved in an experiment, now there was three: 1- The experiment, 2- The instrument of measurement, 3- The observer.

Therefore, consciousness, or at least, the awareness directed at something, interacts with this thing at the subatomic level. This new scientific concept led the way to questions about consciousness and its actual existence.

If consciousness could alter the way matter behaves, then it was obvious it was the same with the mind, and possibly the spirit.

Dr. John Hagelin leads experiments involving the reduction of crime in various places, using only thought processes in deep meditation. A large group of people are gathered in a place where there is a high level of crime, or war, and while everyone is in deep meditation, the level of crime, or war casualties, drop significantly. This experiment was lead more than 50 times with success, at the moment that this book was written.

Considering what was discovered so far, it is obvious that we have the ability to influence the course of events, as much as the behavior of subatomic particles. That is in the nature of the Unified Quantum Field, or the Supreme Consciousness.

The Unified Quantum Field

At the smallest level of observation, it seems that there are no more particles. Everything seems to be unified in a single field of continuous ... stuff,... and non-stuff. The Unified Quantum Field is where everything takes place, where everything starts to exist. Between the atoms, while we think there is void, in fact, is not a void at all, but a completely fill continuous field of energy at the highest possible level of vibration. Yet, it also seems to be vacuum space.

Imagine the Unified Quantum Field on a single plane, with a wave function altering its shape.

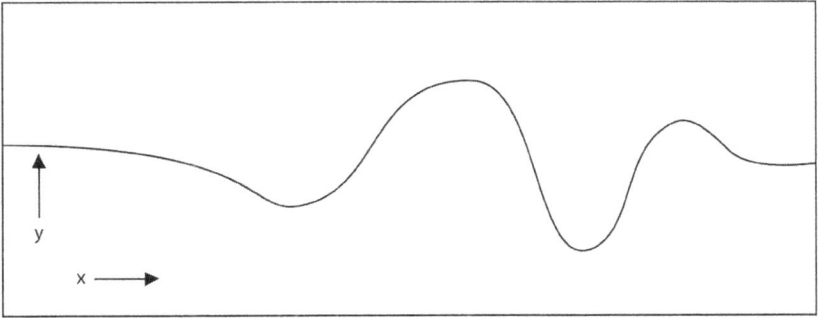

Now, if you could imagine that this alteration is possible not only on a two dimensional plane, but also in a three dimensional volume. On the following diagram, imagine the ticker part of the line closer to you, and the thinner part is further. We used a shadow to help you visualize the line in 3D space.

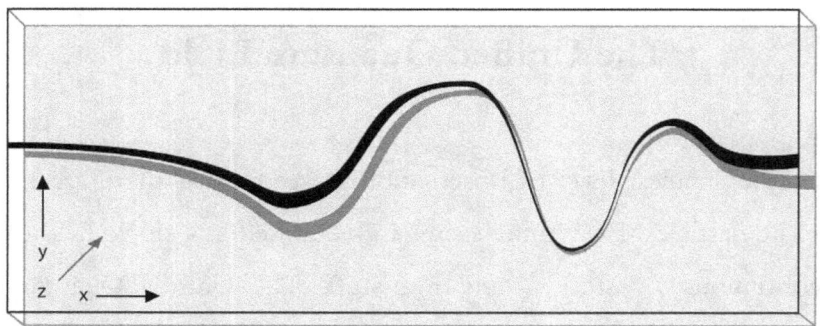

In theory, each of these wave functions offer a certain amount of possibilities of results, where the actual result and shape of the equation will only be defined when the wave function collapses to offer one of its possible result.

Using the planar and cubic wave functions above, try to imagine how the planar 2-dimension wave became a cubic 3-dimension wave, by pulling a new dimension into existence. If you can isolate this concept, then you might grasp the philosophical concept of pulling into existence many more dimensions interacting continuously together, with wave functions made of an infinite number of variables, offering an infinite amount of potential shapes and results.

The main experiment of the Unified Quantum Field is the experience of life itself. We exist within the quantum field. We literally live within this multi-dimensional continuous field of possibilities. More so, we are made out of this field. All that we do as well as all that we are made of, is the result of the collapsing of quantum wave functions happening in the quantum field. The quantum field is absolutely everything.

The Unified Quantum Field is for science what the Supreme Consciousness is for spirituality. Each wave function of the multi-dimensional quantum field is a thought of the highest nature in the Supreme Consciousness. Each of these supreme thoughts comprises the whole of an experience of life. Every parameter of a human thought, a signal in the nervous system, an action, an interaction, a sensation and the awareness of the experience is a single equation summed up as a quantum wave function that is self-contained within all its parameters.

The actions of the body and the body that move are part of a single quantum wave function finding an answer by collapsing to its possible end result. It's like saying that the body, the action of breathing, the thought of breathing and the air that is breathed is the same thing, modulated thru a complete life experience, occurring as a single thought of the Supreme Consciousness.

When we observe life, from the point of view of the human experience, base on our sensory tools, we see everything as separated and compartmentalized. Yet, from the point of view of spirit, beyond the human identification to our senses, everything seems to be united and continuous.

This unification is also possible to observe, using scientific tools and deduction, when we try to look at the smallest occurrences of matter. Yet, scientifically observing the micro-universe does not alter our human perception of life because we are still focusing outwards. To alter our human perception of life, even to alter our senses and our ability to perceive unity directly with our mind, we must implicate ourselves in awakening our consciousness at more refined levels of thoughts, until we become aware of the Unified Quantum Field, the Supreme Consciousness.

From this elevated point of view, not only do we alter our perception of the world, but we also become aware of being the observer of life. Before we awaken our higher consciousness, perception is explained as a series of signals happening in the nervous system, interpreted by the brain, sustaining the belief in separation form the outside world. Yet, when our higher consciousness is awakened, these signals still occur in the nervous system and the brain. However, these signals are not interpreted anymore by our human register of past experiences. When we awaken to the Supreme Consciousness, the being that we truly are is in charge, and the interpretation of life is transported from the manifested human experience to the un-manifested observer, the Spirit. The information is then made available again for the human experience to continue in an awakened fashion.

This information is much more refined than intellectual knowledge. It is pure wisdom of life, information at a level of thought not possible for the nervous system alone to produce. It is an interaction between the observer and the observed, the creator and the created. From the point of view of the human, Spirit is higher and separated from the body, while from the point of view of Spirit the actual human experience is united with the thought of the experience itself.

Wisdom and pure thought is continuously interacting with the material world, in this sense that it IS the material world, as well as the experience of it. Matter and thought are the same from the point of view of the spirit. The coming in and coming out of existence of thought, matter and movement is a continuous dance of quantum wave functions operating the experience of life. This wonderful dance of pure wisdom exchange is made available to the human entity thru the quantum interaction that occurs in the brain.

Creator, Created, Interaction

When we contemplate the nature of the universe, trying to understand it purely, without any reference to already existing dogmatic or scientific concept, we generally come with a first set of observations

- Something exists, thus it is created
- Something created this, or it comes from somewhere
- There is interaction between creator and created

In most of the religious and scientific sets of beliefs, there is a trinity composed of a creative force, a created substance, and an interaction between the creative force and the created substance.

For the Hindu, the creator of all things is Brahma, all that is created is Vishnu, and the transforming force of the universe is Shiva. The Christians classified it in another way, but still we have the Father that created everything, the Christ who is the son and creation of God, and the Holy Spirit establishing a relationship between both Father and Son. The Egyptians have Osiris, Horus and Isis. The Jewish have Eheieh, Iah and Yahveh. It is possible to find the concept of a creator, of a created and of a relationship, in all original observation of the universe.

If you ask a scientist what created everything, where everything comes from, he will say "Energy, everything comes from energy". Ok then, let's ask the same scientist to describe all that is created. He'll say "Matter, mass, that is all that is created". Now how about the interaction between energy and mass? Isn't there movement, calculated in speed, and frequency, often represented by light? All right then! We have a creator, a created, and an interaction.

I can easily imagine a Christian priest making the sign of a cross, while saying "I bless you in the name of the Father, the Christ and the Holy Spirit". The Hindu Brahman would bless us "in the name of the Brahma, the Vishnu and the Shiva". You can as easily imagine a man with a white laboratory gown, basing everything he knows on the name of the Holy Trinity, blessing you "in the name of E equals M, C, square!!!".

Like every other religious system of beliefs, modern science has its Holy Trinity: $E = mc^2$.

Please take a moment to contemplate it. Using their system of beliefs bases on objective observation, the scientific community wishes your well-being, tends to your needs, try to heal your wounds, to alleviate your pain, to make your life easier. I see priests in big churches, faithful to a God with no name. This is quite appreciable.

If you can expand your perception, both the scientific and spiritual communities share the same goal. They are both in a quest for Truth, each using their own means. If we wish to find harmony in all these different approaches towards the concept of Truth, we should start by accepting all systems of beliefs without judgment. From there, we can delve into the system of belief we prefer, and start our real quest for Truth.

Buddhists don't have a God that will come to save them, nor do we pray a single great being "out there" hoping that it will come "in here" to answer our requests. We do not believe in the concept of separation of the "out there" from the "in here". We believe that there is infinite potential everywhere, and that we are all responsible for our use of it. We don't declare there is no God, nor that there is one. If there is a God, then it is all that there is; hence not giving it a definition similar to other religious systems.

However, we believe that everything comes from somewhere, that we describe as a Supreme Consciousness shining like an Infinite Light. This teaching was given by the Buddha, and is called the "Pure Land" teaching, where we dwell in this conscious infinite light, without asking it anything. Conscious Infinite Light in Sanskrit is spoken: Amitabha Buddha. This would be our creative concept. Amitabha Buddha is not a human being that we pray, but a concept that we invoke in our mind, by reciting its name.

Pictured as a Buddha statue, Amitabha is always seconded by two Boddhisattvas, namely MahaSthamaPrapta on his left, and Avalokiteshwara on his right.

Our created concept would be great-powerful-wisdom, or Bodhisattva MahaSthamaPrapta. All that comes into existence is a form issued from the conscious knowledge of that form. Both action and shape are the result of the same quantum wave function. Thus, power and wisdom brought together in a great unified concept, we get MahaSthamaPrapta.

Our interaction concept would be the Lord of the Beholding Eye, or Bodhisattva Avalokiteshwara. This is the "observer" that experiences life. It is the Supreme Self expressed in all forms, conscious that it is observing itself, from its creator aspect looking towards its created aspect. This Bodhisattva is often prayed in religious forms like if it was a real human being. However, it remains the concept of the interaction between the creative and created concepts. It is both the actor and the object of the action; the observer and the object of observation. From this concept, Avalokiteshwara was named the Bodhisattva of compassion, working to save all living beings. It represents the highest point in our individual consciousness, where we merge back with the single united ALL consciousness.

Introduction to Quantum Buddhism

Quantum Buddhism is an adaptation of ancient Buddhist teachings to a new era of scientific emancipation. Quantum Buddhism is not necessarily science, but it certainly is Buddhism. Based on the latest scientific discoveries made in the field of quantum physics, a new form of Buddhism is born.

One of the most important teachings of the Buddha is the Lotus Sutra. The second chapter of the Lotus Sutra is called "Expedient means". This chapter teaches us that we must adapt the Buddhist teachings to each new situation that arises, so to get the fastest and most efficient way to teach the Dharma. The third chapter of the Lotus Sutra is called "Simile and Parable", encouraging us to find ways to teach the Dharma in forms that will make it easily understandable. Here is an excerpt from this chapter, while the Buddha explains this wisdom to his disciple Shariputra:

> « Moreover, Shariputra, I too will now make use of similes and parables to further clarify this doctrine. For through similes and parables those who are wise can obtain understanding.
>
> « Shariputra, suppose that in a certain town in a certain country there was a very rich man. He was far along in years and his wealth was beyond measure. He had many fields, houses and menservants. His own house was big and rambling, but it had only one gate. A great many people, a hundred, two hundred, perhaps as many as five hundred,

lived in the house. The halls and rooms were old and decaying, the walls crumbling, the pillars rotten at their base, and the beams and rafters crooked and aslant.

« At that time a fire suddenly broke out on all sides, spreading through the rooms of the house. The sons of the rich man, ten, twenty perhaps thirty, were inside the house. When the rich man saw the huge flames leaping up on every side, he was greatly alarmed and fearful and thought to himself, I can escape to safety through the flaming gate, but my sons are inside the burning house enjoying themselves and playing games, unaware, unknowing, without alarm or fear. The fire is closing in on them, suffering and pain threaten them, yet their minds have no sense of loathing or peril and they do not think of trying to escape!

« Shariputra, this rich man thought to himself [...] 'My sons are very young, they have no understanding, and they love their games, being so engrossed in them that they are likely to be burned in the fire. I must explain to them why I am fearful and alarmed. The house is already in flames and I must get them out quickly and not let them be burned up in the fire!'

« Having thought in this way, he followed his plan and called to all his sons, saying, 'You must come out at once!' But though the father was moved by pity and gave good words of instruction, the sons were absorbed in their games and unwilling to heed them. They had no alarm, no fright, and in the end no mind to leave the house. Moreover, they did not understand what the fire was, what the house was, what the danger was. They merely raced about this way and that in play and looked at their father without heeding him.

« At that time the rich man had this thought: the house is already in flames from this huge fire. If I and my sons do not get out at once, we are certain to be burned. I must now invent some expedient means that will make it possible for the children to escape harm.

« The father understood his sons and knew what various toys and curious objects each child customarily liked and what would delight them. And so he said to them, 'The kind of playthings you like are rare and hard to find. If you do not take them when you can, you will surely regret it later. For example, things like these goat-carts, deer-carts and ox-carts. They are outside the gate now where you can play with them. So you must come out of this burning house at once. Then whatever ones you want, I will give them all to you!'

« At that time, when the sons heard their father telling them about these rare playthings, because such things were just what they had wanted, each felt emboldened in heart and, pushing and shoving one another, they all came wildly dashing out of the burning house. »

In this story, did the father lie to his children? Or did he find a way to get his message thru? Is the goal of communication to be right about something? Or is the goal of communication to get a message through? As long as we speak the truth, shouldn't we find the best possible wording to address ourselves to whoever we are communicating?

Following the guidance given by this little story, we wish to teach the Dharma in new ways that are adapted to this new era of modern technology and scientific discoveries. But how would we go about? Which scientific field would accept spiritual concepts such as consciousness and Self? The answer arose with the advent of quantum physics.

The quest for truth was once done in churches and temples. But in this new era, the quest for truth is done thru objective observation in laboratory-like environments. Lately, within a few of these laboratories, it was found that consciousness, or at least the act of paying attention, influenced the behavior of particles.

More so, it was deducted that particles are not tangible if someone is not paying attention to them. Particles seem to remain in states of absolute infinite potentials until some attention is given to them, where they then collapse into a single form of their innumerable possibilities. From these scientific discoveries, we had found a way to explain tons of Buddhist concepts such as:

- Consciousness
- Self and non-self
- Unity in all things
- Illusion and Reality
- Impermanence, and more

However, science is based on the supremacy of the intellect holding knowledge of its observations, while Buddhism is completely based on the practice derived from the knowledge. While some of the scientific elite likes do contemplate the accumulation of knowledge, we Buddhists insist in going further to transform one's life. This can only be achieved if we do a practice, like a discipline, that is based on the highest wisdom.

About the Amitabha Sutra

The English translation of the Amitabha Sutra is available on our website, in the member training section. It is a much imaged text, and its reading is more a meditation than a concise teaching. It is not required to read it in order to understand the following concepts. (www.QuantumBuddhism.org)

According to the teachings of the Buddha, one can simply sit in meditation, mindfully reciting the name "Amitabha Buddha" over and over again, while softly contemplating its meaning. One could also recite a salutation like "Namo Amitabha Buddha" or "I welcome the Infinite Light Awakened". In either case, this practice will eventually bring you to become aware of the Pure Land, or if you wish, the Unified Quantum Field.

In the Amitabha Sutra, the Pure Land is described as a land filled with riches and wealth, offering all that one could desire. It is filled with Buddhas and Bodhisattvas, great beings, saints and common beings, all united in a single fully awakened consciousness. If you wish for something, you can obtain it in Amitabha's Pure Land. You simply have to connect to it.

When you concentrate on something for so long, it eventually comes into existence. Some say that in order to connect to the Pure Land, you have to recite the name of Amitabha Buddha for seven days without interruption. Others say you must recite it daily, everyday, to remain connected. Some Pure Land Buddhists mentally recite his name constantly while awake, whatever they are doing. We suggest you first try the meditation, and then find your own application of this wisdom. One thing is certain: if you think about the Unified Quantum Field long enough, you'll become aware of it, and you will even consciously exist into it.

The original Hindu Buddhists recite the name of Amitabha Buddha in Sanskrit. However, the teaching was translated in each other language where Buddhism went, sometimes with only the name, other times with the salutation. Thus, many Pure Land traditions recite the name of Amitabha Buddha in their own language, according to their own tradition:

Chinese: Amitofo
Tibetan: Hoddpagmed
Japanese: Namu Amida Butsu
Vietnamese: Nam Mo A Dzi Da Fa

You can feel comfortable reciting the Pure Land name in the language of your choice. In Quantum Buddhism, we like to recite the Sanskrit name alone. Although, the author of this book experienced high levels of pure thought by reciting the Japanese version since he evolved first thru a Japanese Pure Land tradition called Hongaku Jodo.

The Conditioned Mind

Since our birth, we have been thru a series of experiences that allow us to grasp what is life, if we pay attention to it. However, we also received instruction that conditions our mind into structured thought processes. These mental structures permit us to exist in community, thus they are essential, but they also prevent us from seeing beyond them. We learned about numbers and their strict rules of application. We learned about letters and their strict rules of combination. From this, we learned how to read and count, but we also learned how to encase our mind into a fortress of knowledge, blinding us to the true nature of things, giving only a few openings to see the limited ranges of the wide possibilities life offers.

In Buddhism, there is a teaching about illusion that is often misinterpreted. The Buddha also thought a lot about reality and the pure perception of it. But most uninformed Buddhists simply say that everything is an illusion, which is not what the Buddha said. This leads the Buddhist students to confusion as to what is real and what is not.

Let us take an example at how we are thought about the notion of colors, when we are young. A rainbow shows us a complete range of possible colors. There is no separation between each color. The rainbow is continuous.

Using the grayscale image above, please imaging a continuous color range of light. On a color scale, we put worded labels where the colors seemed to be the most obvious. Red, yellow, green… we put tags on the scale to refer to colors, and in no time, we start forgetting that it is a scale of infinite possibilities, while we keep referring only to the colors where we put a label. Of course, if you go into a pain shop, you'll find thousands of labels referring to as many colors. But when we are kids, we are first thought only a few colors, and that by mixing them, we end up with another set of colors. Quickly, we forget about the range of colors in the rainbow, and we only look at the colors where we were told there was a label. If you ask a kid to describe the colors on a rainbow, he will simply spit out the structured set of labels he was thought, and he won't even understand the concept of a continuous range of colors unless we explain it to him. Because of his conditioning, he only sees the colors we told him about, and refers to them like if there was a separation between each of these labeled colors.

The same goes with time. Time flows in an un-separated continuity. In order to become more productive, we decided to put labels around a circle, using numbers as a structure, so that we could do things at the same time.

We created a system along the continuous line of time, so that we could become more efficient in whatever we do. However, within only a few generations, we forgot that we are the ones who put these lines around the circle, and we started to become enslaved by the system that we previously created. Most of us are no longer using time to remain in a state of mastery over their production means, but are encased in the structure of time.

Was the universe created from 9am to 5pm, Monday thru Friday? Is the flow of life so tight in time with any other species than the human? In fact, does anything else in the universe flow according to what the clock reads? Time is a concept that we created to understand each other, that we enforced to become more productive, and that we now fear. That is what we mean by "illusion". Right now, it is not really the 28th of may 2008 at 4:02PM while I am typing this line of text. However, this is how I would express it to another human being inquiring about it.

We have to keep using words to refer to colors, and numbers to refer to moments, or else, we would not be able to understand each other, let alone work together. However, we must strive to become free of the system, not by rejecting it, but by regaining control over it. Our systems are meant to empower us, not to enslave us. Until we can look at absolutely everything in terms of possibilities, we are encased in a fortress of definite and limited options.

The outstanding amount of conditioning we have acquired since birth goes way beyond words and numbers. Everything we perceive with our senses is categorized, labeled and classified within our mind. This behavior creates a schism between what is perceived and the experience resulting form its perception. No wonder most humans feel anguish and despair. We look at life while remaining separated from it.

If you wish to gain the true knowledge of what is "Time", you have to stop looking at a clock, and turn your attention inwards. While breathing softly in a natural manner, pay attention to your experience of time. Do not dwell in an intellectual recitation of what you thing about time. In fact, try not to think at all in terms of deduction and comprehension. Rather, contemplate your experience of time. Breathe softly and feel. Be aware of what is the flow of time. Experience it in a conscious un-worded thought. Try your best to keep your mind silent, and be mindful of what is time. It can take a while for your thoughts to go down. It can take another while for your mind to start experiencing time in an un-separated, continuous flow. You will succeed in experiencing time out of the illusionary perception when you are spontaneously filled with a rush of life, or happiness, that you cannot explain. This can only happen if your mind is calmed, and if you spend enough time not counting time, paying attention to the pure experience of it.

The same goes with colors. Imagine a complete range of colors while trying to relieve your mind of its references. Contemplate the un-worded experience of color in a single unified range of infinite possibilities. If you start counting colors, or thinking about specific colors, you are not doing it right. Don't think about it, simply contemplate it with no thoughts. Eventually, your entire visual perception center will be purified, and you will start seeing the reality of color, not the illusion of it.

If you practice yourself at perceiving all things in a united, continuous and infinite range of possibilities, you will eventually awaken to what reality is.

Control, Power, Manipulation

In our habit of managing everything in a compartmented way, we have developed a need to control everything. Everyone according to each their own system of belief, will try to control each situation they face, so that they may bring about a stronger sense of security. This need for control is the result of our insecurity. We wish to avoid suffering, and we use drastic ways to prevent it. However, these drastic methods go beyond the control of immediate situations. While we are un-awakened to reality, we wish to control absolutely everything.

When we do not control a situation, or the information regarding a situation, we will try to regain control by using power. The only thing that can prevent the un-awakened mind to use power, is the fear of a more intense opposing power, that threatens to apply pain. Thus, rule number one about avoiding suffering comes back into play. In order to remain in control of a situation, or at least to remain in control of our level of suffering, we learn when to use power in order to gain more control, and when to refrain from using power, so to keep the lowest possible level of pain.

However, we humans have another tool for situations when power simply won't work. It is manipulation. Manipulation is still another defense system that we use to gain more control over various situations, when raw power simply won't work. We have all been thru situations when we start to make up plans to try to get a hold of a daily life situation. Manipulation is yet again a method used by the un-awakened human, hoping to gain more control, in order to avoid pain.

Control, power and manipulation are the ways of war. They always end up in painful situations. The outcome of their use is always the perpetuation of suffering. The main reason for this is that these behaviors are the result of attachments to definite separate definitions of our existence. When we wish to possess something that is not ours, when we wish to receive more reconnaissance than we deserve, when we wish to receive more attention than what we worked for, or when we want to be compensated more for our work… these situations result in producing attachment to things, feelings, emotions, and it results in producing pain.

The source of any conflict is our attachment to their object. The only solution out of this battle is to look inwards at our attachments, and to try to understand them to the best of our ability. Yet, understanding will not suffice. We also have to feel our attachments, and feel their resulting conflicts. By allowing ourselves to feel all that is related to each experience of suffering, we become free of the enslavement of the object of attachment.

Why then don't we just delve into ourselves and resolve every suffering in our life? The answer is simple: fear of the unknown.

Fear of the Unknown

What we fear most is what we do not know. The only way to resolve any type of conflict is to look within and become fully conscious of all the emotional implications of this conflict. The first hint to every conflict is to ask ourselves: what am I attached to in this situation? What do I fear losing, or not gaining?

Paying attention to what we fear losing, or yearn to acquire, implicates that we look at the core of our motivations. A normal human being has no idea about what really drives his decisions. We are more used to react to built-in stimulation than to really think about each and every choice we make. Even when we believe we are spending a lot of time thinking about something, we are not even noticing that what we are thinking about is how much suffering we hope to spare. We seem to be thinking about the goods and bads of each alternative, but we mostly are comparing levels of suffering depending on the various types of attachments we keep in our lives. Yet, we hide this level of reflection to ourselves, sustaining the belief that we are in control.

If we were to look straightforward into the heart of every situation, we would immediately pay attention to what we are attached to, and to what is the resulting suffering. Why don't we do this? Fear of the unknown. Where we are not in control of the situation, we fear. Looking inwards, and simply the act of feeling something inside us, we try to avoid. We wish to avoid feeling something that we don't already see inside us. While we are unaware of what lies inside our mind, heart and body, we fear what we could find out.

However, it is only by going inside to feel what is there, that we can acquire the knowledge of it. The solution to all our suffering is to delve inside, without knowing what we will find, and to pay attention to whatever comes up. This requires faith, and it is possible. With practice, looking, thinking and feeling what is hidden inside of us actually becomes fun. But at first, we have to face the dark and jump.

Its like standing dry next to a pool filled with people playing and having fun, and the only thought that we have in mind is "I hope it won't hurt". Well, the apparent thought seems to be "I hope it won't be too cold", but the real underlying thought is about the fear of possible suffering. Eventually, you simply have to jump in to notice that the water is quite easy. Then you start having fun.

Then, how do we start looking and feeling inside?

Fixity

The technique is simple:
- Can you sit?
- Can you look?
- Can you breathe?

Ok then, if you think you can sit, look and breathe, then do just that! Nothing else.

Sit on a chair or cross-legged on the floor, look at the floor by fixing a point, and pay attention to your breathing. Easy enough? Try 20 minutes in a row, and you'll discover yourself a bit. Most people to who we suggested doing fixity could not bare more than 5 minutes at first. In time, you get the hang of it and you can stare in fixity for an hour.

During the practice of fixity, don't use any mantra or visualization. Don't have background music. Don't stimulate your mind in any way. The goal is to bring the mind to a rest. Simply pay attention to a point on the floor, and to your natural breath.

When you first train at fixity, your mind throws out the trash. Your mind will be pulling out any kind of stuff to try to get you out of fixity. Your eyes will start to move around uncontrollably, and your breathing might become harder. This is normal. Your mind is used to continuous stimulation, so it simply obeys the law of inertia, trying to perpetuate its movement. Whenever this happens, simply keep fixing a point on the floor, and relax your breathing.

When you notice your mind starts to follow a single thought, nourishing a mental fantasy, come back to your non-thinking attitude, and keep being aware of the stuff that your mind is pulling out. Simply come back to the simple thought of contemplating your natural breath moving up and down, in and out. While you are aware that your mind is throwing thoughts like crazy, remain calm and at peace. The goal is eventually not to think anymore, but you have to accept that this is not the case at first. Try not to think, but don't judge the thinking.

Before your mind stops, you will eventually go thru other stages of purification. Actually these are fun, and produce nice feelings inside your body. While doing simple fixity, contemplating your breathe naturally going up and down, your entire energy system is revitalizing. You might feel tingling sensations here and there. These are precursor to more impressive power surges from your nervous system, celebrating its new freedom.

Going further in any other explanation is useless, since it requires the experience of it to understand it.

Releasing the Mind

Non-Human Thought

Thoughts are not limited to the nervous system, or to mental processes. Usually, our thoughts are based on the object of our senses, but this is not the only way to think. There is a possibility to have a pure thought, not based on anything. Doing the fixity practice for long enough, you'll eventually have this pure thought, simply knowing that you are observing yourself, without any other type of mental presence, but the mental presence itself.

Some say everything is energy. Others say everything is thought. Others will say everything is something, like matter or mass. The fact is that everything is made of this one thing that cannot be defined in itself, but is applicable to all perception of it. It you see it as energy, it will seem to be energy. It is the same with thoughts. We like to refer to the pure essence of all things either as Light, or pure thought.

This primordial matter/energy/thought, which is the same thing, will exist and manifest itself in phenomena of various levels, frequency, or density, whatever the way to wish to look at it. The manifestations of this primal essence of all things range from the absolute heights of un-manifested spiritual Self, to the gross and dense material properties of tangible mass.

The thought density scale

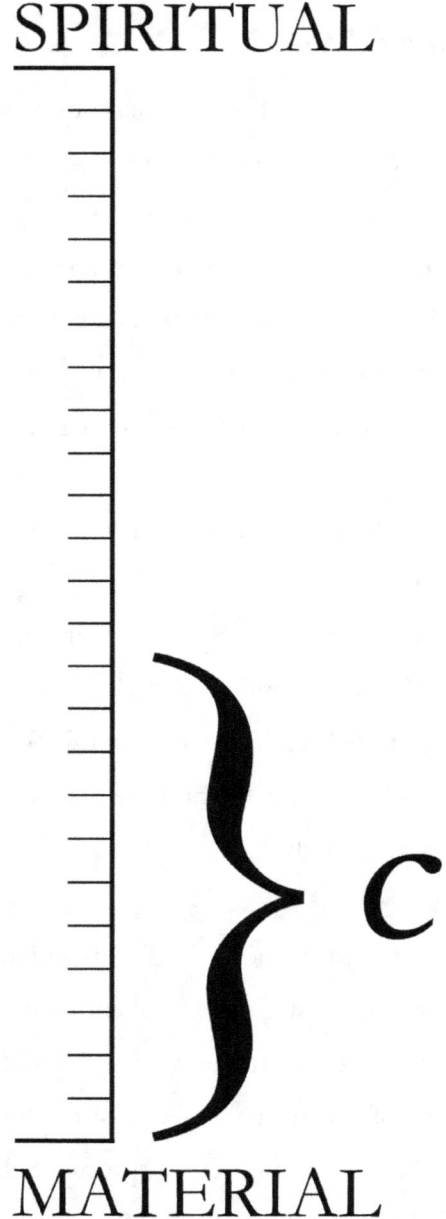

On this scale, we placed the separators anywhere on the scale, simply to demonstrate that there are pointers along the scale. But like we did with the color range, there are no separations along this scale. The various frequencies and densities of thought, light or sound, are not separated. Many traditions will separate this scale in 7 bodies of light, 14 bodies of light, or in the typical western approach: physical, vital, emotional, mental, causal... etc. We do not wish to promote or reject any system. We don't wish to address a specific system at the moment, but rather show a unified way of looking at creation and existence.

On the scale shown here (left page), there is a bracket } showing the lower end of the scale, closer to the material phenomena. In this case, the variable "c" will show the range of awareness of the events occurring along the scale of density. This is the normal range of awareness that we have, in our daily life, more aware of the material events, some emotional and a few mental. In our normal state of consciousness, we tend to limit the perception of higher level events.

When we meditate, or practice fixity, we tend to elevate our range of consciousness so that we start to perceive less information from the material level, and more from the spiritual levels (right). The more we gain experience with meditation or other spiritual practices, the more we become aware of higher levels of thought, light, mass, energy... and the more our range of awareness will expand, covering a broader range of awareness.

The goal of any meditative practice is to get you to become aware of reality as a whole, retaining awareness at every level of the scale, from the material to the spiritual world. This range of awareness is present to fully enlightened (nirvana) spiritual masters. Keep in mind that we can all achieve this goal. A part of the Buddha's teaching is about the fact that we can all achieve enlightenment.

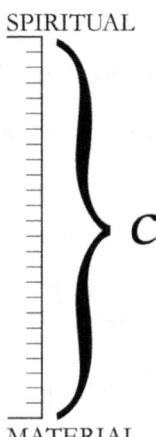

There are various ways to expand our range of consciousness. The most efficient is fixity, but takes the most courage and discipline. There are much more fun ways to do it. The lasting presence of our human ego during the practice of spiritual techniques can be compared to a wall setup around the Self. By playing with the ego, we can learn how to climb over this wall, and have lots of fun during the entire process.

Climbing the Human Wall

Overwhelming the Mind

The key to climbing along the human wall, up to the Self, is to overwhelm the mind with things to play with. Instead of thinking of our ego like an enemy, we rather think of it like a friend to play with. These tools will be called: mantra, mudra, mandala, chakra and dharma. They can all be used separately, or combined together.

Using these playful tools makes it much easier to climb the human wall, until you know how to remove the human wall, or purely perceive that it doesn't exist at all. However, trying to convince yourself that the human wall does not exist is useless, since it is your human wall that thinks this way. Until you gain the experience of the Self, with clear thought based on no object of the mind or senses, you have to deal with the wall, hopefully in a playful way.

Mantra

A mantra is a word, phrase or paragraph that is repeated over and over again until the wisdom that it represents appears in your mind. Before you can consciously exist into pure thought, you need human-level means to produce the apparition of pure thought in your mind.

A sample mantra that we have already covered is "Amitabha Buddha". However, there are lots of mantras that can be used, each for their own specific goal. Repeating a mantra is like doing fixity, but instead of focusing on nothing (which is the hardest part) you keep your focus on a mantra. This will make your mind a bit more at ease.

Let us use the peace mantra, in Sanskrit:
Om Shanti Shanti Shanti.

Repeat the mantra of peace over and over again, for long periods. The goal of using the peace mantra is to bring your mind to eventually accept to think about nothing. You can practice for 5 minutes in a row, on a daily basis, and it will produce its results in a while. If you recite the mantra daily for 1 continuous hour, the results will show within a few days. It is up to you to decide on the speed at which you wish to receive the benefits of the practice, depending on how much determination you have.

Mudra

A mudra is a simple gesture made with the hands. The body is filled with nerves that carry electricity, but it also has a more subtle circuitry, known as meridians. These meridians are commonly used in traditional Chinese medicine in the application of acupuncture. They are also the base of many massage techniques, since they have many beneficial influences on the body and the mind. Their use normally induces a state of relaxation, making the body prone to recovery.

In this case, we will use a simple mudra that is known to produce harmony, by balancing every type of energy in the body. Hold all your fingers together, touching at the tip, like you see on the photos below.

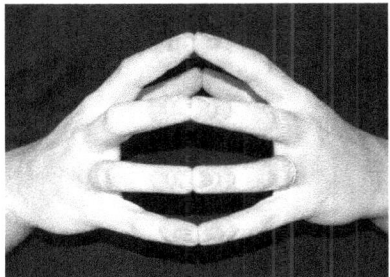 

You can use the mudra of harmony by itself. It consists in practicing fixity, and while you breathe, paying attention to the energy flowing in your fingers, then in your entire body. Yet, this mudra is so much more fun when you also recite the mantra of peace in your mind, giving two stimulations to your mind.

Mandala

A mandala is either a drawing, or an image that you keep in your mind. We will use the mental image in the form of visualization. Mental visualization is there to help us keep our attention on the technique, hoping to prevent the mind to wander too far astray. Yet, if you start to think about random subjects, do not put pressure on yourself to come back to the visualization, but try to come back in a peaceful and relaxed attitude, calmly resetting the imagery in your mind.

The image kept in mind will assist in placing our attention on the focus point, but it will also use colours in ways known as chromotherapy (colour therapy), combining the psychological effect of the colour to enhance the efficiency of our practice period. Of course, the visualization itself will have a subtle reference to the philosophical concept held in mind. These visualisations are suggestions, and will vary from one tradition to another.

In this case, you can visualize a blue layer around your body, radiating with white light. Along with the mudra of harmony and the mantra of peace, it is yet a more powerful technique.

Chakra and Dharma

As for chakra and dharma, there are a lot of books on the subject. Let us say briefly that a chakra is an energy center in your body, where energy tends to circulate. For this technique, you can pay attention to the hands making the mudra, or put all your attention at the top part of your head. As for dharma, it is wisdom, doctrine and philosophy. Contemplate the principles of peace and harmony while you practice this technique.

From Mind to Reality

The more you contemplate a thought process at the human level, the more this thought will become reality, or rather, the reality you perceive will be modulated in order to approach the object of the thought process.

Clearly, the more you think of something, the more it will happen. But it is not only a question of thinking about it, but also a question of "existing" as it. For a thought process to be strong enough to come to exist in your material range of awareness, you have to nourish all aspects of this concept, at every level of the scale of thought/energy density:

- Pure thought
- Mental human definition
- Emotional feeling
- Actions in the physical realm

It is hard for inexperienced meditators to simply exist in a state of pure thought. Thus, we can use specific mantras, mudras and mandalas to stimulate the pure thought, if practiced long enough. These spiritual techniques are available in various formats, and the Quantum Buddhism Association provides this type of training.

The mental definition must be a clear idea of what you wish to create in your life. You must ponder long enough on the object of your desire. Yet, you must also purify your vision about the object of desire. If you think you wish for a big car, but in fact, you really wish simply to be happy, you will not be clear as to what type of experience you really wish to create for yourself. Most of our yearnings are based on the fear of losing, insecurity, and lack of happiness. There is always a mental purification process to undergo before you can really set your mind on what you really want. This purification process will eventually lead you to the detachment from your object of desire.

If you run after a child, even in a playful manner, he will flee from you. But turn you back and walk away, the child will be running after you. Material things behave this way. It is a low of nature. Do not push away what you desire, nor try to attract it with violence. Simply contemplate the design of your creation while at peace, and you will redefine your existence.

The emotional feeling must be in tune with your availability to experience the event in the physical realm. Even if you wish for lots of money with all your heart, if deep inside your mind or your heart you nourish the thought that you don't deserve money, then you will hinder the creative process. It does not mean it will never work, but that the creation process will take much more time to manifest at the level you wish for.

Ultimately, all types of attachments are hindering the way creation happens around you. Non-attachment does not mean "getting rid of", but more simply put "not giving importance to". You can have all that you want in your life, but if you attach importance to objects, they will eventually break or go away, and this will cause you various levels of suffering.

Many people like to think about creating wealth for themselves. They think that wealth will bring them happiness. This is not the case. Wealth only brings excitement. Any type of possession you have beyond what covers for your living needs is superfluous and not essential to happiness. Excitement troubles your mind even more than it is, and makes fixity harder to practice, thus making all types of perception harder to decipher. We are not recommending you get rid of anything you possess. We are not recommending you stop yearning for wealth. We simply suggest that you should seek happiness before any other type of illusionary support for happiness.

However, if you feel you can become happy with a big car, or by having supernatural abilities, or amassing great amounts of wealth, then you can attempt yourself at creating all those things. In the end, you will know if these things really made you happy, or simply excited for a while.

The Formula

The Quantum Buddhists have a formula to express the process of creation. This formula popped into the mind of Venerable Maha Vajra when he came back from meditation. He asked the Supreme Consciousness how he could address himself to the scientific world, and Supreme Consciousness replied with the following concept, in a single pure thought, in ways that it could be explained in the form of a formula. Thus, the following explanation is only a humanized representation of what was purely received in a state of pure thought.

$$I = \frac{ci}{D}$$

A creation, from mind to nature, occurs in a space-time definition. A space-time definition is an area, both in time and space, where natural events occur. When consciously manifesting things or events with our mind, we wish to influence nature. Thus, a certain amount of influence has to be built up before the influence can take place. In this formula, the big "I" will represent the threshold of influence required to build so that the space-time definition can be influenced. The more you think and feel the object of your desire, the more you build up Influence.

The big " D " represents the space-time dimensional area to influence. The bigger the area (D) is, the more Influence (I) you must build up. The denser level you wish to create an influence, the more influence is also required. Space-time definitions are harder to influence if they are defined at a denser level of thought/energy, or at a more tangible level. Thus, influencing matter is much harder than to influence emotions, which in turn are harder to influence than thoughts, and so on.

The little " c " is the range of consciousness that we covered in previous chapters. The broader is the range of your consciousness, the more efficient is the influence. This seems to be the greatest reason why one would want to practice either fixity, meditation, or other spiritual practices.

The little " i " represents the integrity of the consciousness. By this, we mean to point out all the attachments, judgments and other hindrances you keep in your system. The more oppressing patterns you keep in your mind and the more suffering you hold in your heart, the lower will be the integrity of your consciousness. The more you are free from patterns, judgments, fears and emotions, the higher is the integrity of consciousness.

Now that we have covered each variable of the formula, let us explain it again. We prefer not putting numbers on these variables, but if you insist, let's say each variable can hold a value from 0 to 1.

$$I = \frac{ci}{D}$$

Basically put, our integrity (i) is multiplied by our range of consciousness (c), which is what modulates the speed and efficiency of the manifestation process. The greater is our ci, the faster the influence builds up over D. When the threshold point of I is reached, the manifestation can start to happen. This process is not necessarily instantaneous, although it can be if the threshold of conscious Influence can surpass the natural flow of time contained in the space-time Definition. Most of the time, we influence events, thoughts and even emotions, but we rather let the manifestation take place according to the natural flow of time. It can significantly lower the difficulty level of our manifestation process to leave the time parameter out of our Definition to influence, even though more patience is required.

It is not required to understand all the parameters of the formula, or even the formula at all. What is essential to remember from this is that it is beneficial to:
- expand our range of consciousness, by training with various spiritual techniques
- develop the integrity of our consciousness, by taking time to do some form of therapeutic self-observation

Emotional Transmutation

This chapter is included in all books written by Ven. Maha Vajra., since it is of the highest level of wisdom, and is one of the hardest techniques to grasp. It is also considered as an efficient way to develop the integrity of your consciousness. It is similar to fixity, but at the emotional level. While we think it would suffice to write "contemplate your emotion until is disappears into consciousness", it seems this technique requires a bit more guidance, since we are not used to willingly feel painful emotions.

The emotional transmutation technique should not be done excessively at first, but is absolutely required to pursue the training. It can be demanding at first, so just begin by doing it once or twice to get the feel of it. Someday when you feel like exploring your emotional world, you may return to this exercise and practice emotional transmutation more often. You may even wait many years before you perform it regularly. It doesn't really matter right now. Someday, you will feel the need to use this technique. When you do, you will double your efficiency in the field of ESP and supernatural abilities.

When a disturbing experience occurs and you want to resolve it, first take all the necessary physical actions that you must, in order to correct the situation, then you can always work at the emotional level to go thru the entire experience (using consciousness to penetrate the experience and absorb it); by this means you can digest the experience and transform it, thus releasing the need for the experience to manifest physically again and again. This is what some teachers call "the transmutation of karma" or "transcending the human experience". I call this the Transmutation of Emotion.

An emotion is not transmuted by actively wishing it to go away, or trying to get rid of it. Every experience occurs so that you may become aware of it; it is only by consciously becoming aware of the full experience that the emotion will be transmuted and released as a new (higher) experience. We experiment with emotions so that the soul can taste life and so that consciousness can know its own existence. We must not flee from painful or difficult emotions, yet we must not intentionally provoke pain either. This process cannot take place while you listen to the inner voice and its natural fear of feeling pain. You will have to be courageous and go beyond your fear; have faith, release control over the emotional pain and become aware of the emotion without engaging it in any way (not break anything, not hurt anyone, nor yourself).

The Transmutation Technique

Begin the Transmutation Technique by selecting some recent event that you feel guilty about or perhaps some event that left you feeling rejected. You may choose any memory, whether in your recent or remote past, as long as it is not an experience you associate with overwhelming painful emotions of any kind (not for the first attempts). Begin with this problematic but bearable emotion, so you can do the emotional work and still be able to follow along with these three simple steps. Remember that you only need to understand and practice these steps in order to master them.

First step (inner contact): Refresh your memory of the emotion and the situation linked to it. Take a deep breath and feel this emotion without limitation. It is in your belly, within you, and you can feel it more and more. Do not amplify it from your normal stance as the victim of this emotion. Instead, listen to it, feel whatever it brings up for you, taste its flavor, accept its shape and form and how it defines itself (even if that is different than how you were defining it), contemplate it, and hold it within you. Be at peace and relive the emotion for a few breaths, up to one full minute. Be at peace. Later in your training you may perform this with some more powerful emotions. For now, just enjoy peacefully contemplating the positive change you just made.

Rarely, you may feel the need to express an emotion outwardly, in order to release some pressure that seems to be building up. On those rare occasions, (and this is not to be done frequently), simply release what you need to let go of, but never lose control over this experiment. When you are just learning these techniques, it is too easy to revert to victim stance, and to begin amplifying how terrible the situation is. Remember that you are practicing just becoming aware of the emotion. When you are unable to bear the intensity of an emotion, you may release some of the pressure; then just continue on with the process. It is obviously not the goal to keep this emotion trapped inside of you, or buried; rather it is the goal of this exercise to release the hold you have on it. Thus it is perfectly fine to perform the process while expressing some normal human emotion. Simply keep track of the experiment without losing your grip on the process. Breathe into your abdomen throughout the entire process. Do not breathe from your upper torso. Hold the situation that caused the emotion in your mind while you feel the emotion.

Second step (integration): Get inside the emotion and follow wherever it leads you. Breathe deeply and comfortably. As the air flows into your abdomen, your task, as consciousness, is to penetrate the emotion and let it absorb you. Be aware of all the feelings that entering this emotion evokes for you, whether you feel pain or emptiness, coldness or heat, anger or sadness. Get inside of it and become it. The process of Integration requires a conscious fusion of you and the emotion. You are going to allow yourself to be enveloped within the emotion; to be integrated into it. For a few minutes, breathe and accept, breathe and become, breath and feel. Follow the path this emotion leads you on, and you will notice that most of the time, the emotion will be covering another emotion that is buried beneath it.

Every emotion arises into our consciousness because it is linked with some human experience. Use your mind to follow these experiences from the past so that you can remember what happened. You might run thru a few events (while following your emotions), until you come to the first time in your life that you felt that emotion. Stay focused. Do not jump from one thread to another; trace one experience to its root cause, following one thread at a time. As you allow the emotions to exist, without avoiding them or rejecting them, the emotion is freed up, and the energy associated with it ceases to be trapped; the emotion is alive again, emancipated. When you stop blocking it and permit it to BE, your consciousness can understand the profound essence of that emotion.

During the exercise of becoming the emotion, this previously problematic feeling will be re-set to a peaceful, natural state and you will get an abstract but clear understanding of your human experience. You are what you experience, as consciousness, as spirit, as life. Do not rush through your experience of this step. Allow the penetrating fusion to continue for a while, until there is no pain associated with the emotion, only the experience of it. Conscious breathing will also naturally relax your hold on the emotion until it is released. Understand that the emotion will not leave you, it will simply be free to remain inside of you without any of the previous negative associations. Always consciously go beyond your fear of pain; never push away the emotion. With your mind, consolidate the entire experience, which is comprised of all of the life events that made it; breathe and be conscious within that entirety.

The human ego has strong natural defense systems. Many times, the emotion is not blocked all by itself. Instead, the human ego keeps control over it, out of arrogance, vanity, jealousy, and envy, the ego refuses to allow the emotion the right to be resolved, all because of pride. You have to be in charge of this experiment and release the mental hold you keep on your emotion. You simply have to let go.

Third step (liberation): When you feel completely saturated with the emotion you are working on, when your consciousness has transmuted it into a living experience, that emotion (and all the energy that was trapped with it) is freed up. It is not released outside of you, it is available to you again, and all the power and potency of the emotion is alive for you once more. The heavy, dense or contracted energy that was troubling you is released in that it is converted into its essence, and dissolved in your higher consciousness. A good feeling will naturally bubble up from within you. You may feel deeply satisfied, or you may experience a profound state of peace, or you may feel the emancipating joy of freedom. Breathe and allow this new feeling of joy to fill you up, release this positive emotion if you wish to.

After this transmutation, the most important thing for you to do is to contemplate the wholeness of the experience as joyful life and happiness. Even if your physical human experience did not seem to change at all, your inner experience of it became one with the inner Self. Do not let your human ego steal this moment from you. It is crucial for you to rejoice within yourself, for you have tasted life at its fullest.

Conclusion

The more you will contemplate yourself, at every level, the more you will expand your range of consciousness, and purify yourself to reach the highest levels on integrity. To contemplate yourself efficiently (or purely) you have to observe from a unified point of view, rather than from a compartmented system of belief.

While you advance on your spiritual path, you are encouraged to consider the five life precepts thought by the Buddha. During your life, do your best:
- not to kill
- not to lie
- not to steal
- not to have inappropriate sexual behaviors
- not to intoxicate yourself

Most of all do you best not to create suffering, yet you should accept it when it naturally comes your way. Accepting suffering does not mean to let it be, but to allow it to teach you who you are, while you do what is required to be relieved from it.

As of yet, throughout all your life experiences, you have yearned only to become happy. Until now you have fought, or have declined. You have believed in comparison, competition and separation. Yet you strived to become happy. You worked hard to acquire any type of physical wealth, yet all you sought was to be happy. You have attached yourself to people and things, hoping to avoid the pain of detachment, because all you really wish for is to be happy.

From now on, may you find the strength to seek happiness simply for what it is, relieved from the veils of human conditioning, relieved from the weight of desire, and into a blissful experience, may you find happiness, simply for what it is.

I pray that you may find peace, harmony, and happiness.

www.ingramcontent.com/pod-product-compliance
Lightning Source LLC
Chambersburg PA
CBHW062201100526
44589CB00014B/1907